C000193095

To Sébastien and Fabien

IMPRESSIONS
OF AFRICA

Alain Pons

text
Philippe Huet

Africa! A distant, boundless land. An ideal. A forgotten place where we can satisfy our irrational desire for wide open spaces, our utopian need for a lost paradise, an unexplored Eden. A land of musings and fantasies, of great glory and great misfortune. Who, having set foot on African soil, has not dreamt of living the adventure of a lifetime? The kind of adventure that has been told in hundreds of novels and films, of true-life heroes lost on the infinite savannah; discovering fabulous beasts hitherto unknown to man; fighting their way through impenetrable bush to hunt ferocious predators with blood-streaked fangs; sharing frugal meals around the campfire with wise, fierce warriors, whose faces are red with earth; navigating narrow canoes down twisting, churning rivers that sooner or later lead to menacing rapids. What Westerner, however sure of himself or his values, has not felt some inner pull to blend in with these sublime landscapes, to be at one with this unspoiled balance of nature? As the young Dane Karen Blixen, recently arrived in Kenya, wrote to her sister in 1914, '…I have just this instant returned from the depths of the grand, wild magnificence of nature, from life in primitive times, today, like a thousand years ago, from an encounter with the great carnivores that leaves you breathless, swallows your spirit whole, so much so that nothing seems more important than to live for the lion – strengthened by the pure air of the mountains, burnt by the sun, overflowing with the powerful, wild and independent beauty of the dazzling day and the grandiose moonlit night…'

As well as the colonials and the odd adventurer there was, in the first half of the twentieth century, an entire generation of Western hunters who recounted their epic journeys in books with evocative titles such as *The Wanderings of an Elephant Hunter, Jungle Giants, Death in the Long Grass…* Off they would go to Africa, bagging easy-to-shoot big game in order to satisfy who-knows-what vague, unconscious, morbid call to dominate nature, to subjugate 'wilderness'. In exchange for hard cash they also supplied zoos. They killed or captured everything: elephants, rhinos, hippos, lions, cheetahs, leopards, gorillas, antelopes, crocodiles, zebras, giraffes… Assuming the guise of heroes or adventurers, they slaughtered tens of thousands of animals, from Senegal all the way down to South Africa, via Nigeria, Tanzania and Kenya. Alas, it all happened so fast. What we call 'wild' Africa survives only in sparse patches, in areas abandoned by or protected from human presence. The combined effects of colonisation and the systematic annihilation of tribal life,

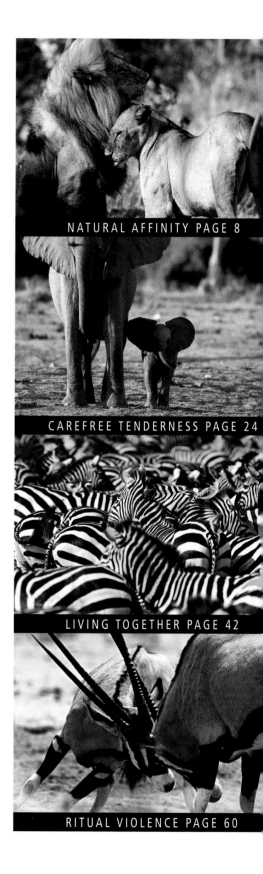

the irreversible loss of species and their habitats, inevitable development, corruption and growing human populations have steamrollered their way through this earthly paradise. In our imaginations, however, the magic of Africa lives on intact, and will linger in our souls for many years to come, as long as we still yearn for wild escapades.

Africa. You see it in the pretty young woman walking along the side of the road, a brightly coloured plastic basin balanced on her head. She is probably heading to the market to sell her meagre harvest of manioc and perhaps a chicken or a few mangos. You see it in the children teasing each other or chasing a ball of rags across a makeshift playground, kicking up grey dust that clings to their legs. Their young captain calls himself Thomas Zidane… In a rickety stall of disjointed boards where an ancient woman huddled on a crate and swathed in a splashy boubou is selling bits and pieces: a cake of soap, charms, a box of matches, batteries, a dried rat, a slice of snake… In a beaten-up old car with worn-out shock absorbers, 15 people piled inside and a radiator grill on which you can still make out the silhouette of a metal lion … In the colourful crush of humanity on the move every morning, busily getting off to a hard day's work, on foot, on horseback, on bicycle, by donkey, by bus, by bush taxi, cart or motorcycle – all singing. You see it in a young man on a bike on his way to sell his dog, which he carries strapped to the luggage rack… In the carcass of a truck in a ditch, rusting in the same spot for 10, 15, 20 years, until it disappears completely into the vegetation… In women by the roadside, their children swaddled on their backs, sweating as they crush yams with massive pestles in heavy wooden mortars. These scenes show everything that is eternal about Africa, everything that is peaceful and certain as well as terrifying and fascinating. But Africa is also the artist shaping clay sublimely at the dead end of a road. A talented cabinetmaker working wood with a gouge and chisel to sculpt a door as detailed as lace. A writer like Chinua Achebe who says in *Things Fall Apart,* a novel that speaks to us all, 'There's nothing to fear from someone who shouts.' A passionate, devoted schoolteacher giving food for thought to a classroom of future sages. A mechanic on the roadside deftly removing the engine of an old four-wheel drive to overhaul the cylinder head with an unlikely scrap of metal. A distinguished old gentleman, incredibly statuesque with leathery, chiselled features, his eyes narrowed by wrinkles, his beard well trimmed, who calmly asserts,

'One day you will return here, to my village.'

'Are you sure?'

'Yes. God wills it so.'

And then one day, at the end of a trail, at a bend in the road, sometimes, for some, the shock hits. The instant when you are intensely, absolutely bowled over. Something grips you at gut level – a deep, aesthetic, emotional reaction to the sheer beauty of the place. As far as you can see there is savannah, an infinite sea of grass, dancing, bowing, waving like wisps of fine hair. The picture is both minimalist and imposing. A buried memory of the original, primordial Eden springs forth. Suddenly you feel that real life is here, in this frenzy of vegetation where nothing has changed since the beginning of eternity, even though you can't say when eternity began, or where it ends. You have the idea, precise yet contradictory: the place is marvellous, absolutely sublime, untrampled by human foot, unspoiled by human presence. And yet, here you are, on this very spot, savouring, relishing a view of bygone times. You are defiling it by your mere presence. But no matter, since you are the first, you have become what came before, you are at the very beginning of it all. For Africa is at the beginning of everything – that is all there is to it.

The savannah floats languorously, moulding itself to the shape of the gentle slopes that hem in the horizon, enveloping everything like a thin green overcoat. Feathery white scarves escape from a vast, clear sky, light as a hornbill's feather. On one side of the picture the artist has painted a solitary tree, a small, symbolic acacia, no doubt thinking, 'This tree will be useful for a passing bird, one that might be tired after a long flight, wanting to perch, to rest for a moment, to catch its breath.' At this precise moment there is no bird, but it will come: tonight, one day, tomorrow? Further on you make out a river. The savannah has formed a barely perceptible wave; its gentle lip seems to roll out in even loops, fading into the motionless landscape.

There is something of the absolute in this image, and enduring fullness. As if things, creatures, plants, the world, should never change. As if everything should remain as it is, beautiful, perfect, unsoiled, virgin. If only it were possible to suspend time, to fix this eternal image in your memory, deep at the back of your eye, to engrave it on to some rot-proof medium. But the scene is evolving. The artist has taken up his brush. Evening has descended and the hornbill feathers have come together in a shifting bouquet. They absorb each other, blending and melding before parting again. Then, slowly, gradually, they form large white clouds that weigh down the limpid heavens. Suddenly everything has turned purple. There is purple in the furthest reaches of the sky, purple in the branches of the acacia, purple in the waters of the river and its even loops. The savannah is as purple as a Warhol painting. The whole picture is smudged with purple. 'A work of art must be a provocation,' the French poet Louis Calaferte observed. And how right he was! Africa itself is just such a work of art; even its colours are provocative. 'Can that purple exist in nature?' you wonder. Well, yes, it can. It does. Here, on the African savannah, in that inferno-like sky where organdie clouds billow, where no bird alights on the purple acacia, where the river has turned to ink. It cannot be denied. You can even, if you wish, imagine it as a negative. Africa can get away with it. For Africa is just as beautiful and seductive in black and white.

Then there are the creatures that live in this idyllic landscape. That is the second shock. The other visual emotion, perhaps even more violent than the first, no doubt because it is a scene both beautiful and carnal. Imagine… In the distance, steamy heat waves hover over the savannah as far as the eye can see. The sun is at its zenith, the atmosphere might be embalmed with ylang-ylang. Nothing moves. Then, there in the evanescent, searing waves, a long, shimmering snake appears. At first the image is blurred, indistinct, stretching the length of the horizon, as if the painter had chosen watercolours instead of oil or acrylics. The reptilian form seems to advance, to hesitate, to thrash, as if stuck in the nebulous, transparent waves. Gradually forms take shape and the true nature of the snake is revealed: a vast herd of wildebeest. They stir up ochre dust as they advance; their brutish heads hung low to the ground, swinging to the beat of their mechanical progress. There are thousands of them. A scattering of zebras accompanies them on their life-or-death journey. They are heading to where the savannah has turned green again, where they know they will be able to feed and give birth, to ensure the perpetuity of the long snake. A vast, breathtaking, unique watercolour.

Then you must take in the details, assimilate little by little the way the savannah – and the creatures that have inhabited it for thousands of generations – live. You must cover vast stretches of Africa, watching, observing, waiting, and waiting longer. One evening in the Masai Mara in Kenya, a leopard, supple and sure of itself, sets out to hunt at the foot of a hill. Nearby, Thomson's gazelles stamp nervously as, out of the corner of their eye, they watch the handsome predator approach at a rolling gait. But they have nothing to fear: the cat is simply heading to the tree into which it earlier heaved its morning prize: a young gazelle. At dusk on the opposite bank of the Mara River, in Tanzania's Serengeti National Park, a herd of elephants emerges from the brush, their thick skin suddenly splashed with the violent dying light, living, tangible symbols of the dawn of the world. At Etosha, in Namibia, at the end of the dry season, an amazing crowd throngs around the last of the waterholes: zebras, kudus, giraffes, oryx, springboks, elephants, jackals, sandgrouse, bustards all come to quench their thirst, their bodies gathered in a star shape around the stagnant puddle, though lions lie close by in the shade of an acacia… What else can they do? In the Okavango Delta in Botswana, a tawny eagle, staunchly positioned on a branch, awaits the toing and froing of doves that come to drink at the river.

It does you good to try to understand these tenuous relationships, the interdependence of casual acquaintance that inextricably binds wild animals to each other. It is also good simply to let the eye take in the unique vision of their presence, without trying to explain or codify it at all cost. Let Africa penetrate your pores, soak into your eyes, your skin, go wherever she wants to go. Only then will she allow herself to be tamed, but then your happiness will be great. For those who do not take the full measure of Africa's draw will be swallowed up by it. In 1926, in another letter from Kenya to her sister, Karen Blixen wrote, 'Will you help me return to Europe? If I stay here, I shall die…'

NATURAL AFFINITY

The savannah is a place of chance meetings, sheer luck, and desires satisfied – or not. Here among the wild beasts, love stories are played out, couples form, families grow. Others separate, clash, kill or die. It is all guided by instinct, intuition and emotion, by thousands of innate urges buried deep within, the result of thousands upon thousands of years of evolution, yet triggered at a precise instant in every animal's life. The lion must seduce the lioness. He cannot do otherwise: his instinct as a male drives him uncontrollably towards the final coupling. He must pass on his genes, father other lions, so that his bloodline, his group, his species will survive and succeed him. Of course, the lion does not read books on behaviour by Boris Cyrulnik before drifting off to sleep. He has known what he must do for all eternity. The lioness, wily and languishing, has shown the male she is receptive. Here and there she has imbued the savannah's grasses with her pheromones, tickling the lion's nostrils, driving him mad with desire, drugged by these imperceptible molecules. His is a physiological response. He approaches her. Licks her. Circles around, then mounts and penetrates her. Not for long. The act itself lasts 15, 20 seconds at most and yet it encapsulates the whole, universal story. It involves everyone: the tiny bee-eaters, perched on their branch in a neat row; the Kori bustard, misunderstood by his mate; the topis with their strange, antediluvian allure, and the vultures. All are captivated by the sexual whirlwind that blows night and day over the savannah. All are guided, possessed by this prodigious instinct for survival.

Left. An unchanging scene witnessed over and over again since the dawn of time: every evening at dusk, little bee-eaters gather and huddle together, hidden in a vast sea of stiff reeds that protect them against the chill of the long African nights. *Okavango,* *Botswana.* **Below.** The Kori bustard is the heaviest flighted bird in the world: an adult male may weigh close to 20 kg (44 lb). This displaying male appears somewhat disappointed; a nearby female seems indifferent to his advances. *Etosha, Namibia.*

The grand ball of the black-crowned cranes. These two handsome birds with their delicate, silky plumage perform a lengthy dance on the savannah. It is an odd display of love: tender, light, airy and almost silent. The only sound is the soft swishing of their long sumptuous feathers brushing together. *Masai Mara, Kenya.*

An exceptional image: a photographer is not often lucky enough to observe these last tender moments between mother and daughter. The young female will soon become independent and will leave her mother to lead the solitary life of her species. *Rongai, Tanzania.*

Among the tall, elegant giraffes
there is no mating season, nor are
there really any stable, structured
family groups. Courtship is therefore
a year-round affair, with mating
depending on chance encounters
and mutual attraction.
Manyara, Tanzania.

About five days, rarely more, rarely less… This is the window, which may occur at any time of year, when a lioness is in heat. She purrs, groans hoarsely, rolls about with pleasure. Mating, which lasts no longer than 30 seconds each time, takes place every 20 minutes without a break. Because it is more efficient and provides greater security for the cubs, the females of a pride all tend to give birth at the same time, so the males don't have much time to catch their breath! *Masai Mara, Kenya.*

Topis are a species of herbivore closely related to the hartebeest. They live in small groups and their reproductive instinct sometimes drives males to absurd actions such as attempting to mate with females who are already raising young. Naturally, such females do not always consent…
Masai Mara, Kenya.

The klipspringer's love story has
a universal appeal. Once these little
antelopes have paired up, they remain
inseparable for life, never straying out
of sight of their mate in the mountains
where they live. Only death will part
them. *Lobo, Tanzania.*

A ballet of feathers and beaks.
The male white-backed vulture spreads
his wings several times to help him
keep his balance on his companion's
back, without a safety net!
After a few coy movements,
she accepts the male's advances,
under the watchful eye of a rival.
A few weeks from now, she will bring
forth life. *Chobe, Botswana.*

Day dawns on the vast white desert. Palm trees grow here and there, favouring the few damp basins or the random patches of water known as pans. These dry up totally or fill bounteously in accordance with the pattern of the rains or the pounding sun. *Kalahari, Botswana.*

CAREFREE TENDERNESS

The future depends on them. They are the only hope for the perpetuation of their species, and the end goal of the preceding chapter… They are diamonds and stars, the continuity of life itself. Through them, genes will be passed down to yet another generation. In solitary species such as leopards and cheetahs, mothers guard their young carefully. When forced to leave their offspring for a few hours to hunt, they first conceal them in thick brush, in the crack of a boulder, under a stump. The mother draws on all her knowledge, experience and cunning to ensure the cubs cannot be scented or seen. Among large gregarious species – Cape buffalo, wildebeest, zebra – young animals grow up at the heart of the herd, well-protected within the moving mass, a giant cocoon of hides, hooves, bellowing and sweat. When, as with lions or African hunting dogs, the young come into the world as part of a highly organised family group, they are the centre of attention, watched over and educated by all of the clan's adults. Elephants live in particular harmony, the mothers forming strong, lasting bonds with their offspring. Elephant families are primarily a female affair, a matriarchy. Daughters, mothers and aunts, indeed the entire matrilineal line will stay together their whole lives. Hornbills have a peculiar ritual: the female settles in a hole in a tree to lay her eggs. The male builds up the entrance until she cannot get out, leaving just enough room to feed her. The pair's destinies are inextricably linked: if the male dies, the female and their chicks are doomed too. If all goes well, the young will be safe and sheltered until they are ready to fly away. And so life goes on.

In spotted hyena families, females are dominant: a male will always rank below a female, no matter what her status in the hierarchy may be. Females are responsible for educating the young — often sternly, for hyenas are highly aggressive from the start. *Kruger, South Africa.*

Lions are the only truly social felines: females who have given birth around the same time will generally remain together for the rest of their lives. As for the alliances young males form at about the age of three, they last until they are old enough to reproduce. *Moremi, Botswana.*

Does any animal have as developed a sense of family as the elephant? Pampered and cared for by the whole herd, baby elephants live in a serene, matriarchal world, where a dominant female ensures the social cohesion of the group. Around her, sisters and aunts, always alert to the needs of family life, assist in watching out for the young, playing the role of nursemaids. Elephants are constantly communicating with each other, and physical and emotional contact is frequent between members of the same clan. *Masai Mara, Kenya.*

You would think that this lion cub was napping on the rough and wrinkled shoulder of an old elephant! Its tail is hanging down casually, it looks sound asleep, its position is relaxed – everything about it points to a secure animal, slumbering without concern: it knows its family is nearby, resting on the upper branches of the same ancient tree. *Seronera, Tanzania.*

This young leopard's mother is not far
away either. The cub has nothing
to worry about, safe in the high reaches
of the branches. Leopards actually
spend much more time on the ground
than in the trees, which they climb only
occasionally. *Ndutu, Tanzania.*

Leading a solitary life, the female cheetah is among the most attentive to hunt, the cubs often fall victim to the jaws of predators, including

Play allows young animals to get to know each other, sort out their position in the group, test their strength, challenge their opponents, explore and master their environment… Games are a part of every lion cub's early life, preparing it unconsciously for the future, when it will need to fiercely defend its place in the lion hierarchy. *Serengeti, Tanzania.*

Watching the horizon, inspecting the surrounding area, this lion mother is attentive to the least movement, the least noise on the savannah. Her cubs are only days or perhaps weeks old. She knows they are frail and vulnerable. So she takes no risks: for the first six weeks of their life, at the least sign of danger or when she must leave them for a time, she hides them carefully. *Ngorongoro, Tanzania.*

This newborn Thomson's gazelle
is searching for its mother's teats.
While this is a classic picture of
motherly nurturing, one can't help
feeling anxious at the sight of such
fragility. *Masai Mara, Kenya.*

The white rhinoceros's only form of family unit couldn't be simpler: mother and calf. Like its close cousin the black rhinoceros, this species is seriously endangered: from a population of several hundred thousand at the beginning of the twentieth century, today only 17,000 remain on the whole African continent. *Nakuru, Kenya.*

Staggering and trembling, barely able to balance on its frail limbs, this newborn zebra has spent a whole year in the warmth of its mother's womb. The mother will soon lick her baby's coat dry, then suckle it conscientiously for close on a year. *Seronera, Tanzania.*

'The gazelle's grace
Has faded in the dying dusk
Of the valley.
An amber flash
Everlasting in my heart has fixed,
In my heart that bleeds from
                              unappeased regret.
For the fragrance of my unheard dream,
Splendour of the tropical sky,
Has dazzled me all too well for
                              the times to come.'
Léopold Sédar Senghor, *À la mémoire
de Soukeina.*
Manyara, Tanzania.

LIVING TOGETHER

The group, the family, the herd, the neighbours, whoever, wherever… Very few lives are lived alone. At some point, they all depend to a greater or lesser extent on others. Whether it be for protection or for food, in order to love, to grow or to sleep. The wild animals of Africa are no exception. They gather, they congregate, they form alliances. Some live in family groups and hunt together, like the African hunting dogs, bat-eared foxes and lions, and all have developed strategies – more or less efficient – for tracking their prey. Large herds, like those of Cape buffalo, provide safety in numbers when travelling or defending the next generation. Sometimes vast communities gather to migrate from one immense stretch of plain to the next. The ancient seasonal migration of the zebras and wildebeest takes them from Tanzania's Serengeti to Kenya's Masai Mara, where hundreds of thousands of animals assemble yearly. Nurseries form, like those of ostriches and flamingos, making it easier to keep an eye on the young. Groups of vultures survey the lie of the land, sometimes flying at heights of 1,000–2,000 m (3,300–6,600 ft). When one of them spies a carcass, the others are able to join the feast within minutes. Monkeys follow the pattern too. Baboons, the most common of African monkeys, are fairly hierarchical. The survival of each individual depends on the observance of group rules. So they respect each other. They watch out for each other. They even excuse themselves politely, sometimes to the point of self-denial.

A mother and three cubs survey
their territory. Cheetahs are fond
of high spots like earth mounds and
termite hills from which they dominate
their surroundings.

This is their observation post: from
it they can scan great stretches
of landscape, sight a prey and judge
whether or not to launch an attack…
Masai Mara, Kenya.

'We must resist the degradation
of the last great beauty on earth as
well as the idea Man has of the places
he dwells. Are we no longer able
to respect nature, living liberty,
without profit, without usefulness,
without purpose except that it be
glimpsed from time to time?'
Romain Gary, *The Roots of Heaven*.
Seronera, Tanzania.

A raucous brouhaha swells over the lake. One immense, hoarse, never-ending cry fills the air like a bellow from another age. The strong odour, at once sharp and sweet, of stagnant mud mixed with bird droppings wafts like a miasma over the warm waters. It has rained for days on end and scores of lesser flamingos have flocked to the waters of Lake Bogoria in northern Kenya.

Motionless, constantly on the alert,
white-faced whistling ducks pay close
attention to their environment:
an eagle attack can happen quickly,
and it is better to be safe than sorry…
Moremi, Botswana.

The landscape is leaden, frozen in expectation. Rain falls in an even, palpable, misty drizzle, enveloping the horizon in a long shroud of grey and lending a ghostly allure to its trees. Time has stopped in this corner of the savannah, where giraffes have vainly sought shelter under the acacias. *Masai Mara, Kenya.*

African elephants are no more than a shadow of what they once were, due to poaching, the ivory trade, the degradation and destruction of natural habitats…

An estimated 5 million elephants roamed the African continent at the beginning of the twentieth century. Today only 300,000 remain. *Masai Mara, Kenya.*

For lions, the picture is almost as gloomy. From a count of 100,000 in Africa in 1900, a mere 30,000 survive, almost all of them in nature reserves and the large national parks. Elsewhere, hunted mercilessly by herders, they have become very rare. *Masai Mara, Kenya.*

Above. Much as they love hot, dry environments, helmeted guinea fowl are daily visitors to waterholes. *Savuti, Botswana.*

Right. Accused of raiding herds and hunted relentlessly, viewed as competitors by big-game hunters, African hunting dogs have been systematically persecuted since the first colonials arrived. The resulting figures make one shudder: only 3,000–4,000 remain on the entire continent. Within the last three decades alone, they have been wiped off the map in 19 of the 37 countries where they were once found. *Kruger, South Africa.*

Much more heavy-set than their females, male common elands can weigh more than 800 kg (almost 1,800 lb). This in no way detracts from their stateliness, to which their spiralled horns, sometimes as long as 1 m (3 ft), contribute. *Masai Mara, Kenya.*

Hunted for its fur, driven off
by farmers (particularly in Namibia),
disturbed by excessive tourism,
struggling more and more to find
the space it needs to survive

(one family's territory may cover
1,000 sq. km or 400 sq. miles), cheetah
populations have gradually dwindled
to between 9,000 and 12,000.
Masai Mara, Kenya.

'Now, being in Africa, I was hungry for
more of it, the changes of the seasons,
the rains with no need to travel,
the discomforts that you paid to make
it real, the names of the trees,
of the small animals, and all the birds,
to know the language and have the
time to be in it and to move slowly.'
Ernest Hemingway, *Green Hills of Africa*.
Tarangire, Tanzania.

RITUAL VIOLENCE

There they are. Face to face. Like burly gladiators come down to the great arena of life. Sweat and fear and sheer bestial beauty stream down their hides. Planted squarely on their feet, they stand stiffly, as if propped up. Their foreheads almost touch and their flared nostrils drip large drops of mucus into the dust. Their crazed eyes are like shining black orbs, turned round on themselves in dilated sockets. Their long tapered horns crash together, locking and unlocking. Around them, the females stand patiently. By the time the fight is over, an oryx will have won the right to mate... Shortly after this scene, another male challenges, keeping up the eternal combat... 'Non-violence is the law of our species as violence is the law of the brute,' said Gandhi. And yet, this tantalising violence and raw bestiality – however shockingly cruel it may appear – is never gratuitous. Animals confront, challenge, fight and sometimes kill each other, but only from deep-seated necessity, from a vital need to dominate, to gain the upper hand over competitors, to ensure supremacy over the group and to hold on to territory. Among animals there is no deceit, no treachery, no crime against 'animality'. Where there is aggression, when two animals fight and one dies, it is due only to chance, to the turn a battle takes under particular circumstances, never to the will to kill. If there is a law among animals, it is above all the law of life, not of death.

A sudden burst of violence from
the usually peace-loving elephant.
In an instant, this mighty beast turns
into a block of raw rage, an unstoppable
mass of wild and primitive fury. When
protecting the young, an elephant's
trunk becomes a formidable weapon,
capable of yanking up trees.
Once the danger is over, the elephant
calms down almost as quickly.
Moremi, Botswana.

Sumptuously choreographed,
two male giraffes waltz to confirm
their status within the herd's hierarchy.
Their long necks cross and uncross
to the languid, timeless rhythm
of their swaying bodies. Their heads
touch and rub in what seems like
a long, sensual caress.
Etosha, Namibia.

The initial challenge seems interminable. Planted squarely on their long, graceful limbs, sizing each other up with bulging eyes, two male impalas paw the dusty earth with their hooves. Rutting season turns these elegant antelopes into fearsome opponents. They face off, bellowing, clashing horns against horns, jousting for the right to control a group of females and claim a territory all their own. *Chobe, Botswana.*

Below. During a fight, a male zebra doesn't hesitate to bite and kick viciously. The stakes are high: will he or will he not maintain his dominance over the herd's females? In this way, some bold, unyielding stallions can hold on to their position at the head of a group for ten years or more. *Etosha, Namibia.* **Right.** Sometimes the traces of violent conflict are written into a hippopotamus's hide: deep, blood-stained scars tell of wounds inflicted by a rival's impressive tusks. *Seronera, Tanzania.*

Left. Their stance is identical: horns interlocked, muscles tensed and hooves dug into the ground. Identical too are their reasons for fighting. Whether it be topis (above) or Defassa waterbucks (below), males fight for the right to court and conquer females, to ensure the continuity of the species. **Below.** Two male lions challenge each other. Although they look intimidating, such clashes are rarely dangerous. Rather such ritualistic provocation allows an individual to test his strength and check out the intentions of a potential rival. *Masai Mara, Kenya.*

Courtship displays and struggles over dominance are the common lot of most of the savannah's herbivores, including Cape buffaloes (left, *Chobe, Botswana*) and zebras (right, *Seronera. Tanzania*). Such ritualistic confrontation is rarely very violent. More often it allows males to test each other's fighting ability. Most importantly, it is an opportunity to impress rivals and show off one's own strength and stamina. Most of the time, the weakest party gives way before anyone is badly hurt or killed.

Adult male greater kudus can weigh
over 300 kg (650 lb) and their horns,
growing in harmonious spirals,
can reach more than 1.75 m (6 ft)
long. Sometimes the horns of two
combatants lock for good.
Then the fight ends, only for a long
wait to set in; the outcome may
be the death of both animals.
Etosha, Namibia.

Male elephants live on the fringe
of family groups, composed mainly
that mate; younger, inexperienced
males are often violently repulsed

Africa never ceases to fascinate. Almost
everywhere there is some forgotten
corner, a lost oasis where the roving
eye may rest from a distance but where
you don't take the time to go. Even
when you know a country well, you are
aware that somewhere there's a hillside,
a cliff, a bend in a river or a rocky
outcrop where you could lose yourself
at last… but where you will never go.
Kalahari, Botswana.

ON THE ALERT

A long, listless wait. Eyes, patiently fixed, searching the lost immensity before them. A scorching sun pummelling the earth, drying it into cracked shards, geometrical and white. Moments suspended in mid-air, heavy with silence, or perhaps disturbed only by a fly's buzzing. Ears twitching discreetly or rotating imperceptibly like a periscope. Predators reading the landscape, assessing whether or not to take action. The prey species transfixed, the anguished expectation of an attack set down deep in their genetic memory. The bloody tear of fangs closing down, the fear of monstrous pain, with death the only way out. Immobility and patience are fundamental qualities on the African savannah, where there is no room for error. For predators, with their exceptional faculty for analysis, biding time is the key to success. They must weigh their chances, save their energy or simply set aside an interval for rest out of bodily necessity. For prey, success lies in knowing how to gauge distances coolly, to judge when to flee, and to refrain from panicking too readily. Then there are long periods of respite, when time hovers frozen over the scorched plains, when trees seem somehow straighter than usual, and long vaporous clouds hang over the blonde grasses like will-o'-the-wisps rising endlessly from the veins of the earth. For animals, such lulls are not to be wasted. Nature sweeps the slate of time clean. They take advantage of the opportunity to groom, to engage in social activities or simply to get some shut-eye...but never more than one eye, one hoof or claw at a time. Here, vigilance is a matter of instinct.

Sightings of the nocturnal and secretive caracal are few and far between. This amazingly agile cat, with its powerful hind legs, is capable of spectacular bounds of 4–5 m (13–16 ft) in the air, enabling it to catch birds in mid-flight. Though only a middleweight (the male weighs about 15 kg or 33 lb), a caracal can capture animals twice its size. *Samburu, Kenya.*

In Africa as elsewhere, genets are discreet and active only at night. They are nevertheless curious, opportunistic and far from shy, sometimes venturing into lodges or campsites to rummage for food. *Banks of the Zambezi River, Zambia.*

Calculating, patient, observant… higher predators such as lions are whole-hearted believers in the law of least effort. 'The less I do, the better I feel!' could be their motto. Should some wildebeest or zebra appear on the horizon, there is no reason to make a fuss. The predators might as well wait, watch how they behave, decide whether they are headed this way or that. It's all a question of perseverance. *Serengeti, Tanzania.*

The ostrich, like the giraffe, has a major advantage over other animals on the savannah: its height. Ostriches serve as veritable control towers and many an antelope or gazelle, without necessarily knowing the cause of the panic, will flee the moment an ostrich does. *Masai Mara, Kenya.*

When raising six or seven cubs, a female cheetah hasn't a moment to call her own. Most of her time is spent locating the animals she will stalk: perhaps Thomson's gazelles, impala or young warthogs. When she has spotted her prey, she must draw as close as possible. She will usually launch her attack at a distance of about 50 m (50 yards); the chase, at close on 100 km/hr (60 mph), will last no more than a minute. But even such carefully calculated attempts often fail. *Serengeti, Tanzania.*

For impalas, there is only one way
to escape an attacking predator:
outrun it. Fortunately, nature has
endowed this antelope with the build
and muscles of an athlete: impalas
can leap distances of up to 10 m
(33 ft) and heights of 3 m (10 ft).
Enough to discourage any number
of predators… *Tarangire, Tanzania.*

Kirk's red colobus monkeys live on the island of Zanzibar where it rises out of the Indian Ocean, 35 km (22 miles) off the coast of Tanzania.

They frequent the few remaining swathes of tropical forest that once covered the whole island. *Jozani Forest, Zanzibar.*

The long strides of the ground hornbills, reminiscent of prehistoric wild turkeys, carry them on a hunt across the savannah. Eyes constantly on the alert, they are able to spot the slightest movement and in the flip of a beak catch a stunned insect or small lizard. Sometimes they even catch small mammals, such as rats, mice and rabbits. *Kruger, South Africa.*

A symbol of strength and power, the lion is ever-present in human culture. In India, it is associated with the throne of Buddha. In Catholicism, it symbolises Saint Mark the evangelist, while in Judaic tradition it represents the tribe of Judah. The lion is also an alchemical symbol for the philosopher's stone. The ancient Egyptian warrior goddess Sekhmet, 'the one who is powerful', had the head of a lion. Some Roman coins also bear the lion simply as a symbol of…Africa!
Lobo, Tanzania.

Less riddled with symbolism than
the lion, agamas are faithful
companions to travellers throughout
much of Africa. *Lobo, Tanzania.*

'Month after month you may
see morning come over the veld,
yet its new-born freshness
and beauty are things which
you can never become wholly
used to.'
Vivienne de Watteville,
Speak to the Earth.
Serengeti, Tanzania.

EATING TO SURVIVE

An old elephant has died in the soft shade of the geometrical branches of a great euphorbia: the candelabra tree. Five hyenas are busy tugging at the folds in the thinnest points of the elephant's hide, inside the upper legs and belly. You can hear the scavengers' heavy breathing, the snap of jaws clamping shut, skin tearing under the pull of brutally powerful canines, the buzzing of thousands of flies. The putrid odour of decomposing entrails has filled the air. Three jackals wait nearby, stretching quivering muzzles and twisting black snouts toward the elephant. For the moment they dare not approach: at this stage of the feast, the hyenas are in no mood to share. Even lions would do well to stay away. Vultures are poised on the euphorbia's thorny, fleshy limbs; others form a perfect circle on the ground. Sometimes they spread their wings as if to announce their approach, but without real conviction. A stone's throw away, marabou storks are a picture of patience, stiff as posts, impervious to the sweltering heat. When the hyenas have finished their banquet, the onlookers feast on the leftovers. The scramble for spoils lasts no more than four days: by the end of which only the pachyderm's bones remain, along with a few patches of skin and flesh, picked clean and scattered in the dust as reminders of what has been. Within weeks, only the great white skull sits in state under the euphorbia, like a forlorn trophy. With the elephant's death, the pirouette of life has spun full circle. In giving up its body, the huge creature has provided for the survival of dozens of others, summing up with its own flesh a slice of life on the savannah: one must eat to survive.

Leopards both stalk and ambush prey, relying on their sense of smell and keen vision. They wait patiently for the right moment to spring an attack, often hidden among tall grasses. *Kruger, South Africa.* **Right.** A leopard's usual catch is young antelopes or warthogs, but it won't turn up its nose at smaller creatures, including rats, hares and rock hyraxes. One individual on an island in southern Africa has even specialised in fishing! *Serengeti, Tanzania.*

Left. A large carnivorous lizard reaching lengths of 1.5 m (5 ft), the Nile monitor haunts river- and lakesides, damp valley bottoms and marshlands. On the menu: crabs, eggs, frogs and birds. *Okavango, Botswana.* **Below.** The tawny eagle is a skilful opportunist. While most often it catches birds like bustards, sandgrouse and francolins, it sometimes targets dik-diks, snakes and crickets. It also scours flamingo colonies where it feeds on dead birds. *Chobe, Botswana.*

It goes without saying that elephants are big eaters: an adult needs to consume about 200 kg (440 lb) of vegetation daily. But elephants also change range according to season, often following trails that have been in use for centuries. By moving from savannah to marshland, from plain to forest, they vary their diet to include dozens of plants and trees.
Moremi, Botswana.

Greater kudus feed on a multitude of plant foods, sometimes relying on their own special technique: they use their horns to break off branches and bring the leaves they eat down to their level. These large antelopes, particularly the adult males, require a tremendous quantity of food, and many die of starvation when vegetation grows scarce. *Kruger, South Africa.*

Lechwes live only in the swamplands or floodplains of southern Africa, in Botswana, Namibia and Zambia. As always in nature, there is a good reason. Lechwes are fairly slow-moving on firm ground, but quite at their ease in water. Living here enables them to take quick refuge from predators. *Okavango, Botswana.*

Cheetah populations in some African reserves have remained relatively stable, but their future is nevertheless seriously threatened. The drop in their numbers over the past decades has reinforced a tendency to inbreeding, resulting in lower genetic variability. Thus the species no longer has the same capacity to cope with new diseases or significant changes in its environment, which makes it extremely vulnerable. The cheetah may have been granted a stay of execution – but for how long? *Serengeti, Tanzania.*

Above. Black-tailed jackals are opportunistic feeders. While capable of hunting down the delicate Thomson's gazelle or young impalas, they won't turn their nose up at grasshoppers, crickets, lizards and snakes, nor even at the dung beetles that live on the droppings of the savannah's herbivores. When lions or cheetahs have made a kill of large prey, the jackals hang around the sidelines in the hope of snatching a bite, sometimes running into the competition, like this Rüppel's vulture. *Serengeti, Tanzania.*

Right. The African fish eagle is one of the continent's symbols. It can be found everywhere there is water, from lakes and riverbanks to ponds and marshlands. Its characteristic silhouette is unmistakable. *Baringo, Kenya.*

ed introductions to
n world. Light dry heat
altitudes…
storms and, in the morning,
in mist like a Chinese ink
psed populations, amiable
ervile.'
nard, *Croquis d'Afrique*
anzania.

THE SOURCE OF LIFE

Here, a small pool lost in the middle of the parched savannah, far from anywhere. Cautious cheetahs visit it regularly to quench their thirst, sheltered from prying eyes... There, the secret shores of a vast lake, where elephants dip their trunks, bathe and splash in an age-old ritual... Further on, every day at the same time, the banks of a river shaded by palms summon a troop of baboons to a vital, sacred rendezvous. Elsewhere, from first light and for a few days, hundreds of small birds draw life from a puddle in the middle of a dirt road, the last trace of almost forgotten rainfall. Thousands of miles away, a sprawling swamp disappears into the horizon where herds of antelopes and zebras kick up thousands of atoms of life... Life! Since the world began, water and life have been as one. Life derives inescapably from water, it *requires* water. Always more. In Africa, as elsewhere, an animal can go without food for days, even weeks; some, like the crocodile, can survive for months. But without water? Without drinking? Under the relentless sun? As the African proverb says, 'The water of a river never returns to its source.' Time passes, days pass, nights pass. Water flows, sinks down, dries up, absolutely and definitively. But animals remain, as does their need for this vital fluid, this fundamental component of survival, of life. When water is short, when the wait for rain is on, animals save their strength, drawing on their own deep resources. One day, water must return. If drought settles in, animals 'invent' other strategies: seeking moisture in plants, leaves, fruits and roots... Under the blazing sun, they pant, perspire, raise their body temperature, do anything they can to ward off Africa's monstrous heat.

Left. Light of flight, the immaculate egret is transformed into a snowy feather; for an instant, it seems to escape earthly gravity. *Chobe, Botswana.*
Below. Unusually, this solitary female cheetah is drinking at night; these cats tend to be diurnal. Her cubs are no doubt hidden somewhere not far off in the savannah. She takes advantage of the cover of darkness to drink, secure in the knowledge that the cubs are well concealed. *Elephant Plains, South Africa.*

The anhinga belongs to the same family as the cormorants. It too spreads its wings after each fishing session. Scientists say this behaviour doesn't necessarily mean they are drying their feathers; it could serve to regulate the birds' internal body temperature. *Okavango, Botswana.*

Etosha National Park, Namibia:
at the height of the dry season,
the heat is stifling and all the herbivores
assemble near the few remaining
waterholes scattered here and there
across the savannah. Naturally, these
large gatherings attract lions, cheetahs
and leopards. At the slightest hint
of a predator in the vicinity,
the impalas clear out (below).
Sometimes a place at these temporary
poolsides is hard to come by; here
a herd of greater kudu (right) must
patiently wait their turn.

They approach timidly, circumspectly, taking every precaution. Almost sneaking just in case. It's the same never-ending story: is there a predator lurking nearby? The giraffes' reflection in the water becomes a tangible metaphor for their ancestral fears. *Etosha, Namibia.*

Water, the vital element for millions of creatures. Elephants require vast amounts of it. Depending on age and weight, a single animal may drink over 100 litres (25 gallons) a day. From dry season to rainy season and depending on the region, the herds must sometimes cover many miles to get from a feeding spot to a waterhole. *Chobe, Botswana.*

At waterholes across Africa, the same
scene is repeated relentlessly: animals
come to drink, approaching with the
utmost caution. It sometimes takes
a herd of zebras half an hour to reach
the life-giving source. Once reassured
that no predators await them, they
proceed straight out into the middle
of the pool. But should any one
of them take fright, the whole herd
will stampede… *Seronera, Tanzania.*

Below. The Nile crocodile bides its time: its days are generally devoted to loafing in the sun at the water's edge or on dry land, and its metabolism allows it to eat on average only once a week (though if necessary it can survive for up to two years without a meal). *Selous, Tanzania.*

Right. The jacana lives in close proximity to the crocodile (which doesn't prevent the odd one being eaten). This spindly-legged bird has a special liking for stretches of water with floating vegetation on which it walks. *Okavango, Botswana.*

Every year, nearly a million wildebeest migrate from the Serengeti in Tanzania to the Masai Mara in Kenya in search of rich pasture, crossing a tumultuous border to get there: the Mara River. The animals run, trip, trample and knock each other down and drown. Some are devoured by crocodiles, others by lions, African hunting dogs and hyenas... In the final count, 10 per cent of the herd will have been lost along the way.

At the same time every year for thousands upon thousands of years, the waters of the Okavango have swollen, engulfing everything in their path. But, unlike the world's other great rivers, the Okavango does not flow into the sea. Instead it finishes as a vast delta in the middle of the burning sands of the Kalahari.

PORTRAITS OF THE WILD

You can tell every sense is alert, yet he is poised, attentive, almost immobile. His gaze carries far across the immense green and blonde savannah. He studies every detail of the landscape, impervious to the onslaught of heat, wind and rain. Without moving a muscle, he watches as a long column of wildebeest crosses his line of vision. When a black rhinoceros comes near, he does not budge, does not reveal the least trace of fear, though he stands back, on the alert. Near the acacia into which a large male leopard has climbed, he is motionless; he seems to be staring without seeing at the magnificent spotted cat that is finishing off the last of a gazelle killed the day before. He always uses the same trails that criss-cross the savannah; the same dry gulches. Sometimes he penetrates the beautiful forest galleries where liquid sun streams in; other times he works his way up to the top of a gentle hill or rocky kopje. You can tell he knows his territory backwards. There is no doubt that he has travelled these vast expanses for many years now. When an old lion emerges from the vegetation almost beside him, only the twitch of an eye reveals a cautious though real emotion, a slight apprehension. Only elephants cause him any alarm, and even they don't do it all the time. If they are calm and restful he can approach them without too much worry. When night falls, he disappears, to reappear before dawn, before the first mist of morning. Again he begins to stalk, to wander. From time to time, after a pause, he snaps a photo and only then, if he is satisfied, do you see a faint smile. That's all, and it is as it should be.

The countenance of this Cape buffalo shows brute strength and raw power. But there is also a filigree of vulnerability beneath the bronze. For the buffalo, as for other species, life holds no certainties. Whether alone or in a herd, it requires open land in order to survive. And open land is increasingly scarce on this planet, where humans are omnipresent and less and less room is left for true wilderness. *Ngorongoro, Tanzania*.

The gerenuk is a genius of its own.
It lives way up in the north of Kenya,
in Samburu; in Tsavo to the southeast
and in Tarangire in Tanzania – anywhere
that the land is truly arid. The long,
slender neck with which nature has
graced it explains its nickname, the
giraffe gazelle. To reach edible foliage,
this elegant species stands on its hind
legs. The gerenuk is all grace and
beauty… all African. *Samburu, Kenya.*

Could this be a photo from 50 million years ago? Could someone have found it in the dark corner of a long-forgotten cave somewhere between South Africa and Ethiopia, hidden in a rusty chest riddled with worm holes? It hardly matters who took it. Here it is today and in it we can almost see, deep in the recesses of the animal's thick folds of skin, the continuity of its presence here on Earth. *Ngorongoro, Tanzania.*

Above. A lion playing to the camera?
He looks straight into the lens without
a blink, so sure of himself, of his good
looks… His bearing is utterly confident,
his gaze unfathomable. What could
be going through this lion's mind?
Barafu Kopjes, Tanzania.
Right. A giraffe chews on leaves,
her lopsided jaw giving her a comical
expression: a snapshot of nature in all
its simplicity. *Rongai, Tanzania.*

Left. At this precise moment, the elephant is nothing but a mass of raw, unwavering strength. As anyone who has been in close quarters with this mighty beast knows, the overwhelming sensation of power it exudes during a charge makes it seem truly indestructible. Here the action is accentuated by the spray of water all around. *Chobe, Botswana.*

Below. From the look of this lion, even he would appear to have his little day-to-day worries and bothers: a pesky fly, a tick in his ear… *Masai Mara, Kenya.*

Above. There is a mythical quality about the sable antelope, one of the most statuesque creatures on the savannah. To observe it is always a moving experience – and a fairly rare one, as it lives only in southern Africa. *Chobe, Botswana.*
Right. When we see a lion sleeping, stretching or generally lounging about, we cannot help but believe that the notion of pleasure exists not only in ourselves but also in animals… *Kruger, South Africa.*

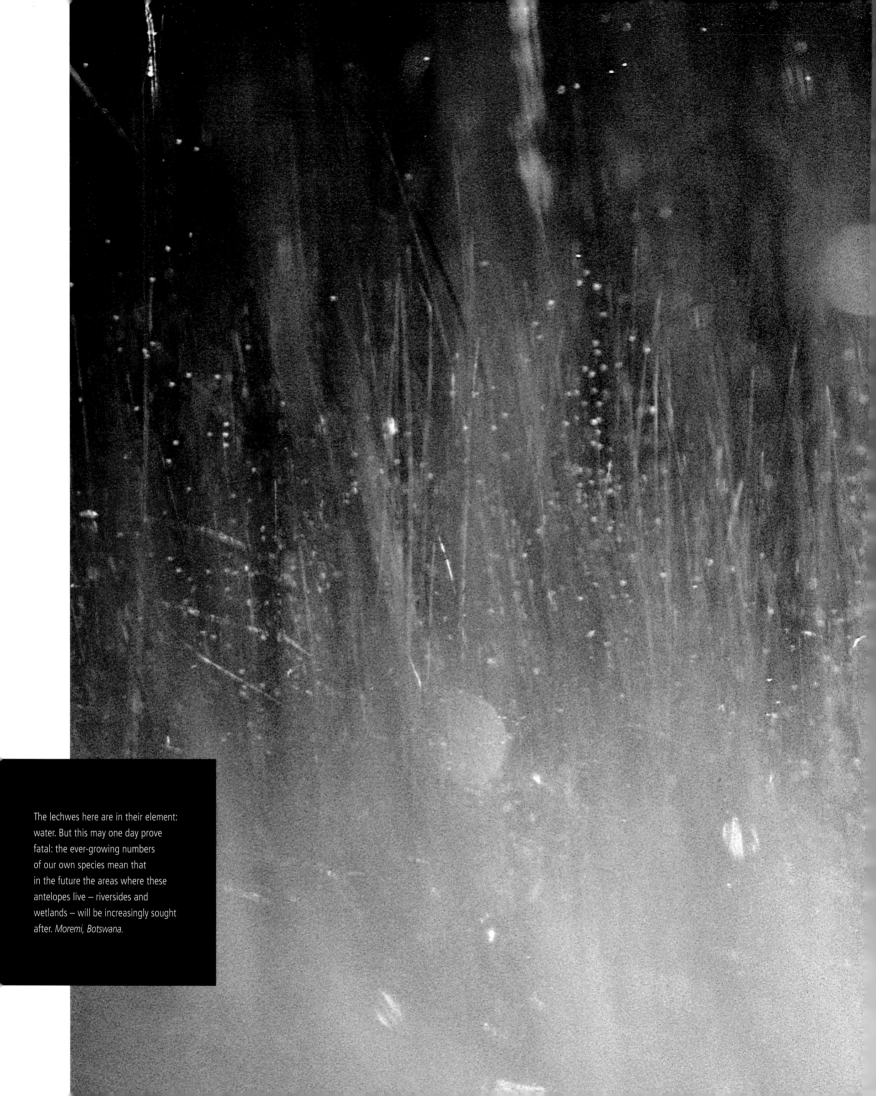

The lechwes here are in their element: water. But this may one day prove fatal: the ever-growing numbers of our own species mean that in the future the areas where these antelopes live – riversides and wetlands – will be increasingly sought after. *Moremi, Botswana.*

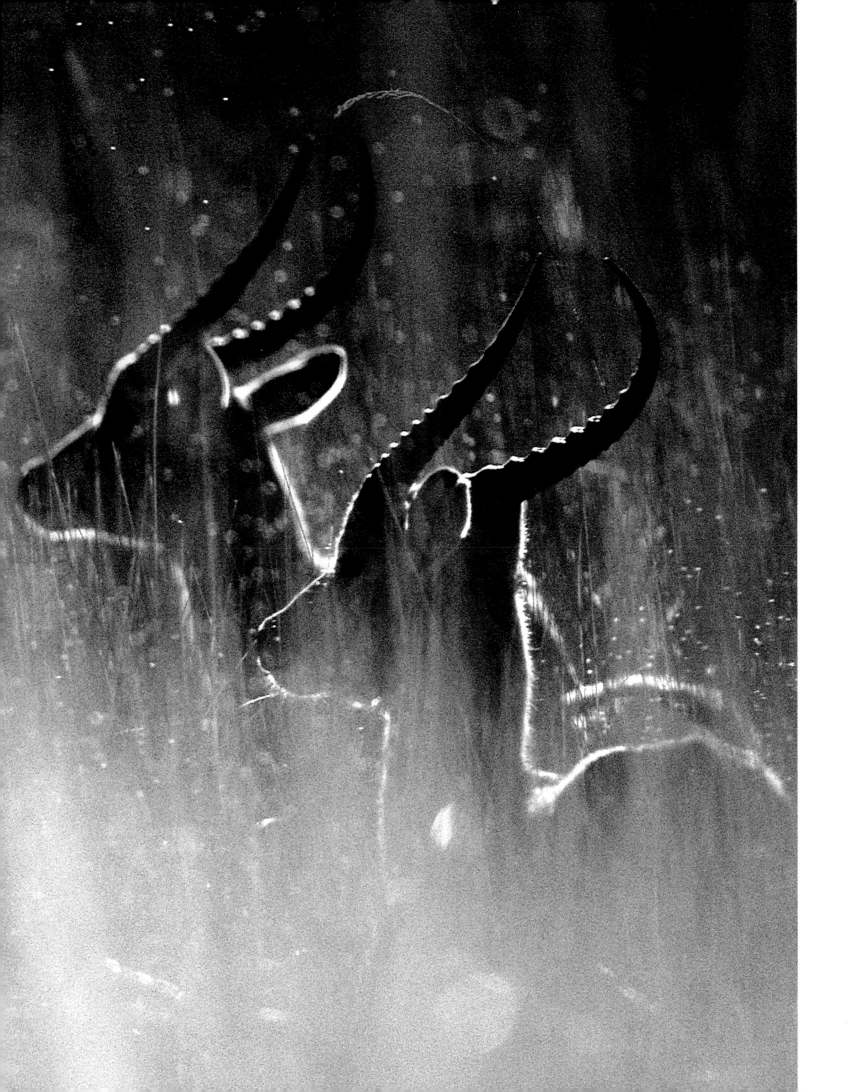

From the outset, the sight of a large bird of prey such as the tawny eagle stirs feelings of strength and power. But then a more subjective, perhaps anthropomorphic impression also emerges: we sense that the bird knows where it is going, sure of itself and its physical abilities. *Chobe, Botswana.*

Elephants, with their massive physique, must constantly regulate their body temperature. Besides spending long periods in the shade of trees, they bathe and shower regularly and flap their ears rhythmically, both indispensable activities for effective heat control. *Moremi, Botswana.*

Yawning is universal. Scientists are still uncertain as to its exact role, but we know its serves several functions. It helps keep us alert when we are bored or about to doze off, and it acts as a form of non-verbal communication, especially among primates like this baboon (below), for whom it helps to relieve social tensions.

The leopard can adapt to a broad range of environments, from burning deserts to mountain tops (leopard tracks have been observed on the snowy peak of Kilimanjaro) and rainforests. This adaptability has made it one of the most widely distributed of the big cats; it ranges from South Africa through the Middle East and all the way to South-east Asia. *Seronera, Tanzania.*

Despite its thickness (up to 5 cm or 2 in), an elephant's skin needs daily care, especially to protect it from parasites and sunburn. Elephants regularly take both dust baths and water baths, the ultimate being to combine the two: first water, then dust. *Etosha, Namibia.*

'When I was a young boy, the smell of the soft air, the sight of wild places and wild creatures, and the sound of unseen animals in the night seeded deeply in me a love of Africa, a love of nature... Nature was and still is cleansing and recharging to what, for want of a better word, I call my soul.' Richard Leakey, *The Sixth Extinction. Masai Mara, Kenya.*

IMPRESSIONS OF AFRICA

First published in the United Kingdom by
Evans Mitchell Books
The Old Forge
Forge Mews
16, Church Street
Rickmansworth
Herts. WD3 1DH
United Kingdom

Photography copyright © 2009 Alain Pons
Text copyright © 2009 Philippe Huet

Graphic Design: Empreinte & Territoires, Paris, France
Translation: Letitia Farris-Toussaint
Editing: Caroline Taggart
Pre-press: Studio Goustard, Vanves, France

British Library Cataloguing in Publication Data
A CIP record of this book is available on request
from the British Library.

ISBN: 978-1-901268-39-3

Printed in Germany